# Tw[illegible]y Elephants

Written by Jeanne Willis

Illustrated by Tony Ross

One fine day when Mum was away,
two baby elephants came to play.

They ate all the food,
they drank all the drink,
they broke all the dishes
in the kitchen sink.

They slid down
the banisters,

they jumped on the chairs.

They danced on the table

and ran up the stairs.

With a thump, thump, thump,
and a crash, bang, crash,
they jumped in the bath
with a splish, splosh, splash.

They scrubbed their backs,
they scrubbed their tails,
they weighed themselves
on the bathroom scales.

They made the towels
all black with mud.
They made the bath
and the toilet flood.

They put their pyjamas on
and went to bed.
"Thank you for having us,"
the elephants said.

Mum came home later that day
and this is what she had to say:

"Who ate the food?
Who drank the drink?
Who broke the dishes
in the kitchen sink?

“Who broke the table?
Who broke the chairs?
Who’s been running
up and down the stairs?

"Why are the towels
all black with mud?
Who made the bath
and the toilet flood?"

"It wasn't us!" my brother said.
"It was two baby elephants.
They're in your bed."
Mum peeped round the bedroom door.
What do you think that our mum saw?

No baby elephants! They had gone!
They left with their pyjamas on.
Mum would not listen to a word
we said...

...until she found their slippers underneath her bed!